KINGDOM OF DAHOMEY

A BRIEF HISTORY FROM BEGINNING TO END

HISTORY HUB

Bonus Downloads

*Get Free Books with **Any Purchase**History Hub*

Every purchase comes with a FREE download!

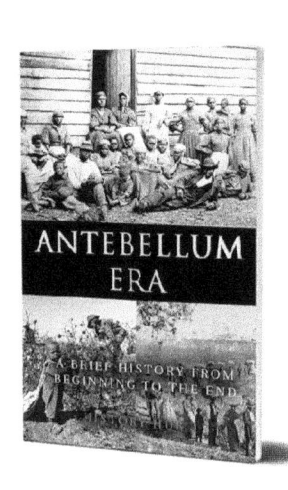

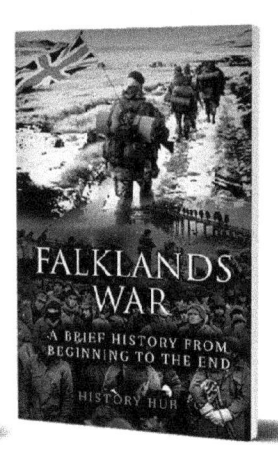

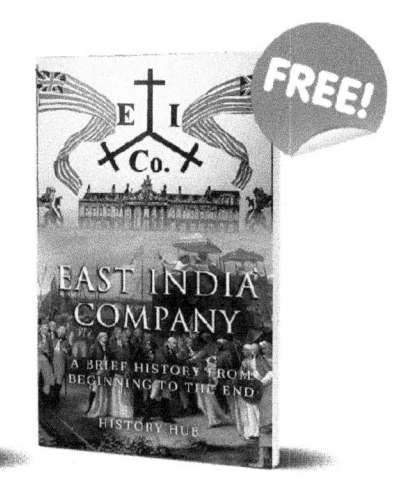

Kingdom of Dahomey

A Brief History from Beginning to the End

History Hub

© 2024 Copyright by History Hub. All Rights Reserved.

Please Note: The book you are about to enjoy is an analytical review meant for educational and entertainment purposes as an unofficial companion. If you have not yet read the original work, please do before purchasing this copy.

Disclaimer & Terms of Use: No part of this publication may be reproduced or retransmitted, electronic or mechanical, without the written permission of the publisher. The information in this book is meant for educational and entertainment purposes only and the publisher and author make no representations or warranties with respect to the accuracy or completeness of these contents and disclaim all warranties such as warranties of fitness for a particular purpose. Product names, logos, brands, and other trademarks featured or referred to within this publication are the property of their respective trademark holders and are not affiliated with this publication. This is an unofficial summary and analytical review meant for educational and entertainment purposes only and has not been authorized, approved, licensed, or endorsed by the original book's author or publisher and any of their licensees or affiliates.

CONTENTS

Part One: Editor Foreword

Chapter One: Introduction

Chapter Two: The Kingdom of Dahomey

Chapter Three: The Dahomey Amazons

Chapter Four: Vodou or Voodoo

Chapter Five: Dahomey Amazon Politics, Language, Culture,

Chapter Six: Colonial Aspirations

Chapter Seven: Dahomey Wars. Brushes with the Legion

Chapter Eight: Defeat

Chapter Nine: The Scourge of Slavery

Chapter Ten: The Decline of Dahomey

Chapter Eleven: Trivia from Popular perceptions of Dahomey

Chapter Twelve: Conclusion

Chapter Thirteen: Discussion Question

Chapter Fourteen: Quiz Question

Your Free Bonus Download

Chapter One
Introduction

Imagine visiting the African Kingdom, the home of the Amazon warriors, the dark heart of slavery, the birthplace of voodoo, and the scary place where ritual cannibalism was practiced. Find yourself in the sultry, warm tropical heat where palm trees grow lush and tall. You're in the Kingdom of Dahomey. Let's explore it.

Dahomey was a historical kingdom situated in West Africa. It was highly successful during the 1700s and 1800s. It's now part of the southern Benin region. The traditional story around the beginnings of Dahomey is that in the early 1600s, three brothers fought for supremacy in the kingdom of Alladah, which had grown rich, trading in slaves. The one brother succeeded in ousting his siblings, so the one traveled southeast and founded Porto-Novo, which is now the capital of Benin. The other, a man by the name of Do-Aklin, decided to go north. He founded the kingdom of Abomey, which later became Dahomey. All three brothers were vassals of the kingdom of Oyo and paid tributes to the Yoruba.

Dahomey existed as an independent state for more than 250 years, from 1625 to 1894. Its name only changed to Benin in 1975.

It was Do-Aklin's grandson, Wegbaja, who made Abomey very powerful. He was followed by Akaba and Agaja. Agaja was a powerful, ambitious man who ruled from 1708 to 1732. With the aid of his terrifying army, he conquered the territories of Whydah and Allada and called the new larger state Dahomey.

The kingdom grew rich and powerful on the back of human misery, making its money from slavery. Dahomey reached its high point in fame and success under Gezu, who reigned for forty years until 1858.

The kingdom was an absolute monarchy. The king's word was final, and he surrounded himself with an impressive retinue. The hierarchical structure was simple. He was at the top with his family as royalty, and almost everyone else was commoners with little say and no power or slaves who did most of the work. The commoners were the bureaucracy, and there was a series of checks and balances to make sure they didn't challenge the king. Each man, away from the central power and ensuring the country was well run, had a female counterpart who kept a check on him and reported to the king. Dahomey had an aggressive policy of conquest and assimilated other tribes by intermarriage, consistent laws, and a general hatred of the Yoruba, which everyone shared.

Dahomey was intent on expanding to acquire more land, become more powerful, and source the slaves that they traded with slave traders. These slave traders made them very wealthy. Dahomey was one of the main gateways for the approximately 8 million people who left Africa as slaves. The enslaved people were also used to working in the plantations and supported the Dahomey royal household and army by growing food.

The army was very active and of particular interest was the women's army, which was called Amazons by the British.

Dahomey continued to prosper until 1840, when the British succeeded in ending the overseas slave trade. Gezu tried to recover by getting his slaves to work on the palm oil plantations and increasing palm oil exports, but there was considerably less money in palm oil than in enslaved people, so the kingdom became poorer. Then after a period of hostilities against the French, Dahomey was made a protectorate of France, its king exiled, and its kingdom and reign of terror ended.

Chapter Two
The Kingdom of Dahomey

Before the forming of the Kingdom of Dahomey, there was evidence that very poor tribes lived on the Abomey Plateau. They were called Gedevi, and without established trade routes and good resources, they merely eked out an existence from the land. They were subject to the powerful Oyo empire, which is present-day Nigeria. There is evidence of some dealing with Portuguese traders, but little is known until 1533, when the Portuguese government signed a trade agreement with them.

The West African Kingdom of Dahomey came into existence from approximately 1600 till 1900. After that, it became a French Protectorate. Then from 1958 to 1975, it became the Republic of Dahomey and is now part of Benin.

Geography

Dahomey was founded on the Abomey Plateau by one of the chiefs of the Fon people in the early 1600s. By the 1700s, it had become a significant regional power. It expanded to the South and conquered important cities like Whydah on the Atlantic Coast. This guaranteed unhindered trade for its most important commodity, slaves. The Atakora Mountains run through part of Dahomey, and it stretches down to the Atlantic Ocean. It's very hot and humid and would have been densely populated with wildlife, which as in all countries of the world, are now largely restricted to Game reserves. At the time of the Kingdom of Dahomey, there would have been abundant hunting.

Economic Significance

For much of the 1800s, the Kingdom of Dahomey continued to strengthen and grow, eventually even ending its period as a tributary of the important Oyo Empire. It was well known to European countries because it was at the forefront of the slave trade. Its domestic economy revolved around conquering neighbors and taking slaves to sell to European traders. As a result, it had an advanced international trade footprint. Its administration was sophisticated and centralized. It had a well-organized, powerful army largely composed of women warriors and an impressive taxation system. Its army was almost entirely utilized in attacks and raids on other nations. It sold the captives from these raids for a motley, although a coveted selection of gunpowder and guns, tobacco and pipes, alcohol, fabric, and cowrie shells. This seems a sad indictment that human life should be so little valued. Captives not required for the slave market were used on the royal coconut palm plantations or occasionally used in human sacrifice.

Annual Customs

Human sacrifice was particularly common at the "Huetanu" or the "Annual Customs" ceremony. King Agaja was a particular fan of these ceremonies, which started around 1730 and involved a whole myriad of entertainment and social interactions, including military parades and religious ceremonies, which included human sacrifice. It was also a time for collecting tributes and giving gifts and for important people to discuss the future of the kingdom and offer advice and ideas. Human sacrifice was an important part of the Annual Customs, and people were sacrificed as a tribute to the deceased kings of Dahomey. Usually, about five hundred slaves were beheaded during the ceremony. At a ceremony in 1727, it was reported that four thousand were killed, but this was unusual. The practice of decapitation and blood sprinkling, Xwetanu, was literally translated as "yearly head business." Some beheaded captives were roasted and eaten piping hot at the end of the ceremony as part of the ritual.

Art

Dahomean art was quite distinct from other styles of African art. The royal family was very supportive of the arts and invested heavily in artists and their work.

A wide range of styles and materials were used, including ivory, wood, silver, brass, ironwork, clay work, and exquisite applique cloth.

Another important form of art was bocio or power sculptures. They incorporated a wide range of materials like wood, bones, fur, beads, and feathers, which formed a figure of a person on a stand. These bocio sculptures were devised to create and unlock powerful protection and other forces. The royalty was often represented in zoomorphic forms depicting their strength and power.

Wheeled carriages, usually as gifts from Western allies, were also used by the Dahomean and were usually drawn by men at state functions owing to the limited number of horses. Some carriages were shaped like elephants or horses, and driving in one was considered very prestigious.

It goes almost without saying that living in or near the Kingdom of Dahomey was probably pretty terrifying unless you were royalty. Life was cheap, and citizens, soldiers, and captives alike would have been exposed to danger and risk of death on a daily basis.

Chapter Three
The Dahomey Amazons

When the Western missionaries and traders first entered the Kingdom of Dahomey, they were amazed to find that much of their army consisted of a group of highly trained and skillful women warriors.

The Amazons

The European visitors were so startled and impressed by this group of warlike women that they called them Amazons after the militant women warriors from Greek mythology. The Dahomeans, however, called themselves Mino. In the Fon language, this means "our mothers." Some of them were also called ahosi, meaning "king's wives."

Their origins are uncertain, but they came into being during the reign of Houegbadja in the mid-1600s. They were originally a group of hunters called gbeto. The number grew from a modest 600 in the 17th and 18th centuries to an impressive 6000 women warriors by the mid-1800s.

They were expected to stay single and dedicate their lives to the protection of the kingdom, giving up everything associated with traditional female roles. The European visitors saw them as masculine, and myths arose that they became men after making their first kill.

Why women?

The early Kingdom of Dahomey was short on men because the powerful neighboring empire, the Oyo, took them by force as slaves. There was also a high death toll because of their penchant for conquest and violence. This led to an increase in women warriors as the women hunters rose through the military ranks. Some of them might have been captives, but many were volunteers. Some girls as young as eight were also recruited. It was also a good place for women who were rebellious or stubborn at home or were not attractive enough to please their husbands. If their husbands or fathers appealed to the king, it could be a one-way ticket to the army for them. The king also disposed of some of his hundreds of wives in this manner if they displeased him.

The Amazon women underwent intense physical training to become fit and tough enough for war. They were taught how to survive in the wild and were trained to ignore the pain by storming through acacia thorn defenses and killing captives. They also had to learn to deaden their "feminine" sympathies for victims of violence and death. They had different areas of skill. Some were experts with a bow and arrow, while others excelled with rifles. They also fought barehanded or with knives and lethal razor-like spears. They wore uniforms that indicated their regiments. Discipline was crucial, and retribution for disobedience was swift.

Women of low status and poverty could use being one of the Mino to improve their social positions and wealth. They were trained to be aggressive and develop masculine traits. Sex and childbearing were prohibited, and a large number of them were virgins. They were seen as partly sacred and treated like minor deities. There's no documented evidence, but oral tradition has it that they were subjected to genital mutilation to help them resist temptation.

The "Real" Amazons

The Mino were named Amazons by visiting Europeans. These were a group of women warriors from Greek mythology portrayed in many ancient legends and celebrated in epic poems. They were a group of female warriors and hunters, superior in fitness and skill to men and able to beat them in areas of combat, horse riding, strength, and agility.

Their society was not open to any males, and they killed any sons born to them or, if they were fortunate, returned them to their fathers. They raised their daughters to be warriors. They only had brief sexual interludes with men for the purpose of procreation. These independent and courageous women followed their queen into battle across the then-known world, Asia Minor, the Aegean Islands, Thrace, Egypt, and Arabia. They were also associated with founding temples and establishing ancient cities.

While there is no certainty that they actually existed, and skeptics have tried to pass them off as men with long hair and shaved beards, there has been significant archeological evidence to show the burial sites of female warriors. In 2019, for example, a grave was found containing many generations of armed women Scythian warriors. It is probable that the Amazon myth had some truth and that women went to war in certain cultures, like that of the Dahomeans.

The Dahomey Amazons are another twist in the tale of the fascinating and chilling world of the Kingdom of Dahomey.

Chapter Four
Vodou or Voodoo

The Kingdom of Dahomey is the home of Vodou or voodoo, as it's been called by those who don't understand it. It's a traditional African religion, and it's managed to survive in the New World. The name Vodou comes from the Fon word meaning Spirit or God. The name is sometimes pronounced Vodoun or Vodoun, but the spelling Voodoo is derogatory and sensationalist and has come to imply simplistic rituals like sticking pins in figurines, hexing enemies, and turning people into zombies.

The Actual Vodou

In fact, it is a monotheistic religion that recognized a supreme being called Mawu-Lisa among the Fon. This religion provides meaning and security in a troubled world, as all religions are meant to do.

Possession, which is one aspect that scares Westerners the most, is manifested by how the great communal spirits, the Iwa, meet with and inform the ritual participants. Through dancing and singing, they become one with the Iwa. The Iwa rides the possessed people, as a cavalier rides a horse, and the chawl or horses, as possessed people, represent renewing the Iwa's stamina during feasting and dancing. The Iwa then communicated with the people who were in need of answers.

Vodou is the traditional Afro-Haitian religion that was left with the slaves through the Dahomey gateway and still survives. It also shows features of being influenced by French Roman Catholicism by missionaries in the 1600s and onwards.

Vodou is a broad worldview that encompasses medicine, justice, philosophy, and religion. Its premise is that everything is spirit. Humans are just spirits in the visible world. In the unseen world, there are the Iwa which are spirits, the mysté, which are mysteries, the zanj or angels, the Invisibles called the anvizib, the ancestor spirits, and the spirits of those who recently died.

The spirits live in a mythical cosmic realm called Ginen. The Christian God created the universe, and the spirits helped him rule the natural world and humanity.

The main aim of Vodou is to serve the spirits and perform various devotions to appease or please the spirits and get particular favors like wealth, health, and protection. During the possession rituals, trances are also common, and the devotee may drink or eat some ritual foods. Cannibalism is not unknown in some cases, but cannibalistic rituals are more often performed as a show of power. The devotees perform specific dances and might perform athletic or sexual feats and medical cures.

The ritual dances, trances, and other aspects of the possession ceremony are meant to restore and refine the balance between spirits and people.

The rituals can usually be performed by both a priest and priestess and must be in the presence of that famous Vodou fetish, the sacred snake.

The color of the sacred snake is yellow and white for some tribes, and it gets offered blood sacrifices from white cocks and goats or milk and fruit, while the deadly green mamba Vidu gets its blood sacrifices from black animals, particularly roosters.

Vodou is also part of a tradition where family spirits led by elders bring rituals to family groups through an oral tradition. In bigger groups like towns, actual congregations are formed, and this spiritual knowledge is passed on through the practice of "kanzo," which is ritual initiation. There is also a great deal of input from ritual drummers. There is normally no formal leadership, with people following where the spirits lead, but some secret societies called Sanpwél and Bizango perform a juridical function. This must be quite terrifying for those brought before them.

Many of the Iwa are practiced in saints' days, which might seem ironic but is typical of the amalgamation of Christianity and traditional religions worldwide, particularly in Africa.

The Modern Face of Vodou

Vodou has maintained its presence in Benin, which was Dahomey, as it has in the Caribbean and other places.

Fetishists or high priests still have enormous influence. As with the Sangomas of South Africa, people come to the fetishists for problems as diverse as barrenness, fears, love issues, and illness. Apparently, even ministers of religion and people wanting a dry garden party or wedding go to a fetishist to approach the thunder god on their behalf. Sacrifices of food are still found at crossroads to be spread by the winds to the gods, and there is a cult house in all villages.

A modern fetishist's practice has a traditional waiting room and a long line of patients who, after being driven to a frenzy by the ritual drummers, enter through the red, white, and black curtain into the fetishist's chamber and, hopefully, find the answer to their problems in the fetishist's champers with its goatskin covered the floor, and its walls draped with charms including human hair.

The fetishist wears a horned red skull cap and has the fetish items in front of him. The client pays his way with some dollars and a bottle of gin, which the fetishist pours over the fetishes as a libation. He then swigs a liberal portion after swallowing a raw egg. He is now part of the spirit world and can offer the required advice. All clients have to realize is no gin, no advice, but if they bring the grog, the spirit world is open to them!

Chapter Five
Dahomey Amazon Politics, Language, Culture

The Dahomey people are also called the Fon, and they speak the Fon language, which is closely related to Ewe, which is spoken by modern-day Nigerians. This language is part of the Kwa branch of the Niger-Congo languages. French is also spoken by the Benin people, which used to be Dahomey.

Political Structure

The villages of the Dahomeans were under a hereditary chief who answered to the supreme king. This was traditionally the main political unit. In the Kingdom of Dahomey, during the 18th and 19th centuries, these chiefs were deputies of the strong king. A major purpose of the kingship was to conduct war, which was followed by the ritual "Annual Custom," at which captives were sacrificed, and the benevolence of sovereign ancestors was sought. The king also exerted judicial power, amassed tributes, and offered political appointments. Usually, members of the royal family did not hold political positions because it was thought there would be a temptation to plot against the king. As a result, crucial posts belonged to commoners who would be loyal because they owed their position to the king.

The Economy

The traditional economic activities of the Fon, as with most traditional African cultures, are agriculture-based, reliant on maize, yams, and cassava, for subsistence living. Palm oil became the main commercial crop after the abolishment of slavery. Men would clear the ground and hoe and prepare the fields, and men and women would plant the crops. The produce would be cared for and harvested by the women. There would have been a cooperative grouping of men to aid in such jobs as clearing communal land and building houses. Each little village would also have a professional hunting group surrounded by supernatural sanctions. There would have been crafters, including men who were weavers and ironworkers, and women who made pottery. Crafters were arranged into formal guilds.

Economic activity was arranged around four-day cycles of religiously sanctioned markets, and the main form of currency was cowrie shells. The complex tax system included officials who went to villages and assessed their population and levels of production, creating a unique tax for each village. The king was also taxed on his extensive lands. The road system was extensive, and the royal roads were kept weeded. Toll booths were set up to impose annual taxes on the goods that people carried along those roads. Public nuisance taxes were also imposed.

The Social Unit

The Fon family social unit was a polygynous unit with each wife and her children living in a home within a family compound. A family lineage, related through the male line, would occupy neighboring compounds. The senior male family member would serve as the head of the family. Patrilineal clans dispersed throughout Dahomey were formerly important, but clan organization has broken down in recent times. The worship of ancestors, however, remains a major feature of the Fon religion. This is part of a complex system of communication with the spirits.

Chapter Six
Colonial Aspirations

Dahomey, huddled along Africa's Atlantic coast, had been a sporadic source of attention from European colonialists since Portuguese and Dutch explorers noted the Gold Coast in the 1500s and 1600s. Dahomey operated a successful slave trade of major interest to the colonists. By 1887, the Dutch had moved on, but the Portuguese maintained lose control over exporting Dahomey palm oil. In 1887, King Glele canceled treaty rights with the Portuguese. This created a trade vacuum that France was very interested in filling.

France's attention to Dahomey was both political and geographic. French West Africa had been growing since the 1870s, and the French colonial office favored a port or two to facilitate movement and Dahomey seemed to fit the bill.

As for political rationale, the French were already irritated with British control of Nigeria, but when Germany imposed a protectorate on Togo, they got really antsy, especially with the colonialist lobby insisting they were falling behind in the race to seize bits of Africa.

The French consul struck the right chord when he advised his leaders in March 1889 that France needed to enter a pact with the King of Dahomey before Germany did.

However, signing an agreement with King Glele was not easy. France set up a minor military and commercial presence on the coast, and immediately Glele told them that he wished all foreigners out of his country. They had come in without an invitation, and they could leave again just as quickly.

Before France could frame a satisfactory reply, the king died, and his son Béhanzin, who was even less diplomatic, took the throne. It was customary for Dahomey's kings to lead their army on slaving excursions. The prisoners were utilized to work in the palm oil plantations, sold as slaves, or apparently were eaten in cannibal rites. When Béhanzin started his reign with a slave expedition into the coastal plateau, the French, pretending to be righteously indignant, took a number of Dahomeanofficials captive. Béhanzin avenged his fellow citizens by taking French captives and attacking the errant town. The attack was repelled, but a month later, Béhanzin's forces tried again and failed again. This time the French and the Dahomeans brokered a deal recognizing some French rights over a few coastal cities in return for an annual financial subsidy. Neither side intended to honor the treaty but needed time to recover their strength.

The next time Béhanzin undertook a slaving raid, the French accused him of trespassing on their agreed territory. They declared war against Béhanzin, who was angry and defiant, asking who had given the French rights over the Dahomey territories. He told the French to carry on with their trade and commerce quietly if they wished to maintain peace. If they wished for war, he was happy to oblige.

Béhanzin's threats were not taken seriously, and within a short time, the French began to assemble troops from the French Expeditionary Force (the formidable legionnaires) on the Dahomean coast.

Are You Enjoying Reading?

As an independent publisher

with a tiny marketing budget

we rely on readers, like you.

If you're receiving help from this book,

would you please take a moment to write a brief review?

We really appreciate it.

Chapter Seven
Dahomey Wars. Brushes with the Legion

The French were determined to make their mark on African territory, so when King Toffa of Porto Novo asked for their aid, they were keen to oblige.

Dodds

The French Foreign legion was called in to suppress the rebellious Dahomeans. They were greeted at Porto Novo by King Toffa, who was wearing a French Naval cap and an embroidered frock coat but nothing else. He was delighted that the French had come to his rescue and offered many porters to assist Colonel Alfred-AmédéeDodds in attacking the Dahomeans.

Dodds was a battle-worn soldier, ideal for African Wars. He had little conscience and was happy to do whatever was necessary to win. Dodds had a small force, less than 4,000 Legionnaires, Sengalese sharpshooters, and some tribesmen from Niger and Sudan. Dodds left a small reserve in Porto Novo and went after Dahomey in three columns.

The Attacks

The going was heavy even though porters were carrying most of the equipment. The heat was stifling as they were in the middle of a tropical summer. They often had to cut paths through mangrove swamps or tall grass.

By the time the column reached the town of Dogba, the men were exhausted, and they rested for some days waiting for stragglers. They built a well-protected encampment surrounded by brushwood, and the riverfront was protected by gunboats. They were satisfied that no one would attack them when the Dahomey warriors took them by surprise. The shrieking hordes of Dahomean warriors rushed out from the forest and assaulted the French. They would possibly have prevailed if their shooting habits had not been so arbitrary. They preferred to shoot from the hip or kneel on wooden stools they carried with them. Fortunately for the French, two other Legion companies joined them, and the Dahomey ground attack was subdued, but sharpshooters in the trees caused havoc until the French launched a bayonet attack. The Dahomeans eventually faded back into the forest. Both sides had experienced heavy casualties.

The Dahomeans had left almost 1,000 dead French men. The Legionnaires examined the Dahomean dead and were amazed to find many women among them. They were wearing their traditional blue sarong with their breasts exposed and a red fez-like headdress. The women were armed with razor-sharp double-edged machete-like weapons and Winchester rifles. The two women captives were shot and burned with the men captives. After the French found one of their men captured by the Dahomeans had been disemboweled and castrated, they had no stomach for mercy.

A few days later, the French expedition continued North, very warily this time. They were attacked by screaming hordes at dawn on 2 October. The Amazons, maddened by British gin and urged on by fetishists, led the attack. The Amazons were relentless. Even if they were injured and disarmed, they would fight with hands, feet, or teeth.

The French retaliation using cannon power repulsed the Dahomeans for a second time.

Chapter Eight
Defeat

The French began the long march to Dahomey. It was a terrible 60-mile walk through storms, mosquitoes, and unbearable heat. The terrain was impenetrable, and thirst became an issue as they were forced to leave the water courses. The Dahomean marksman would attack them if they broke away to fill water bottles.

The Sacred City

Dodds and his men, by October 14, had reached the town of Kotopa opposite the sacred city of Cana, which the priests had promised Béhanzin could never be taken by white men.

Dodds left artillery to bomb Kotopa and took his infantry upriver to try and ford it, but the Dahomeans got wise to that and shelled them until they retreated.

Dodds withdrew his men and set up a camp some distance off in which they could recover. He was down to 1,500 men, many sick with dysentery, wounds, and exhaustion. Many of the porters had run away, and the French were in a sorry state, so they needed to rest and wait for reinforcements.

Unfortunately, Béhanzin did not understand that this was a tactical withdrawal and thought his enemy was defeated. The Dahomeans attacked the French camp with their full force and received the same slaughter from cannon and the tactical French square formation that had driven them off in Dogba and Glele. The Dahomean warriors described the French military strategy as "a great and evil bird who defends itself with its beak in front, with its wings to the sides, and with its claws behind."

The Push

Béhanzin, at this point, decided to opt for negotiation. He was losing the war, there was smallpox among the people, and the slaves in the palm oil plantations were rebelling. Dodds, however, had no interest in that. He said that he would only discuss terms when they reached Abomey. British and German advisors assured Béhanzin that the French would never take Cana.

As soon as his reinforcements arrived, Dodds went on the offensive, burning Kotopa and crossing the Koto River to approach Cana. He knew that the taking of the sacred city would weaken Béhanzin irreparably.

The Fal

The French legion led the attack on Cana. The walls were tall and well-guarded. German Krupp gunners mounted the defense, along with a formidable infantry showing, but by three o'clock, the walls had been breached, and there was fierce fighting in the city. The French lost 200 men, but by morning the tricolor had been raised over the city.

While Béhanzin and Dodds discussed terms strongly in French favor, the Legionnaires wandered through the pagan temples filled with horrifying icons and mounds of human bones.

On 15 November, Dodds marched towards Abomey. There was no fight. Béhanzinhad attempted to set fire to his capital and fled, leaving smoldering outskirts but intact inner courts and temples, which were a grisly sight with human skulls mounted everywhere. The French disgust was rather mitigated by a find of vintage champagne and good red wine, which helped to wash down the revulsion at the atrocities they had witnessed.

Béhanzin eventually surrendered to the French after a few years of lying low and was sent to exile in Martinique, where he lived on a French pension.

Chapter Nine
The Scourge of Slavery

William Cowper, the British poet, wrote these words about slavery, *"I pity them greatly, but I must be mum, for how could we do without sugar or rum?"*

A Trade in Human Flesh

We can't write about the Kingdom of Dahomey without looking at the broader picture of the terrible scourge of slavery. A large reason for the collapse of the Kingdom of Dahomey was the end of international slavery in the mid-1800s. Slavery had been far more lucrative for the militant kingdom than the palm oil trade, which replaced it. Slavery, however, was an immoral, cruel and inhumane way to make a living, and the Dahomeans deserved to lose that terrible livelihood. It is impossible to feel saddened in any way by the demise of the Kingdom of Dahomey.

The Slave Ship

Imagine a group of terrified, exhausted men, women, and children who have been dragged from their homes, beaten, and tormented until they arrived at a harbor where a slave ship stood waiting for its cargo. The stench of death, fecal matter, and decay wafted across the bay to where these terrified people were standing. They were already dreadfully hungry and thirsty, and the children were shaking with fear.

Coins were exchanged, and the little group was handed over to some harsh-looking white men. They were led to a makeshift shelter where they were shackled with heavy chains. They were packed into the hold of the ship with barely room to move. Children were particularly favored because they could be squeezed into smaller spaces. Among the vomiting and diarrhea from sea sickness and disease, no hygiene, insufficient food, and water, beatings and pain, these terrified human beings with no idea where they were going were packed together until they reached their destination, America. Fifteen percent of lives were lost on the ship, and suicide was so common that captains placed nets around the vessel to avoid losing their precious cargo. Even crew members committed suicide or ran away to avoid being exposed to such terrible brutality.

And in the end, there would be a lifetime of servitude on an American cotton or sugar cane farm. Sugar cane was a particularly harsh crop to work and the lifetime of a sugar cane worker was seldom long. It did not matter, though, because the Amazon soldiers of Dahomey were busy, halfway across the world, attacking and capturing a fresh batch of commodities to send to the sugar cane farmers.

The sweetening of tea and coffee was more important than human life, and this established the tone for American slavery and provided the market which kept the Dahomeans in power.

Where does the blame lie? With those who created the market, those who transported the commodity, or those who provided it? Certainly, those who bought slaves to America and other countries receive most of the bad rap nowadays. Still, the people of Benin, who are the remains of the Kingdom of Dahomey, should not be held without blame either if one's seeking accountability.

Chapter Ten
The Decline of Dahomey

During the 1840s, Dahomey started to face an economic downturn. This happened for three reasons.

The end of the Slave trade

From the 1840s slave trade was on the decline. Slavery had been abolished in England in 1807, and pressure mounted for it to end internationally. The British had been major purchasers of slaves, but this was no longer their policy. Instead, they wished to pursue a more active policy of African colonization. The British tried to persuade King Ghezo to abandon the slave trade but continued to resist. In 1851-1852, a British naval blockade was imposed on the Dahomey ports to force them to end the slave business. Ghezo signed a treaty with Britain in 1852, accepting the end of the slave trade. He also ended large-scale invasions of his neighbors and human sacrifice, but this only lasted until political pressure caused him to renege on this deal. He resumed both the raids and the slave trading. He was assassinated by an Abeokuta sniper, which caused the two countries to resume hostilities. Nonetheless, the end of slave trading was in sight, and even as he reduced slavery, Ghezo increased the palm oil export business. Unfortunately, this was never nearly as lucrative as slavery had been, which led to the weakening of power and economic hardship in the Kingdom.

Defeat from Abeokuta

Dahomey was weakened by a significant military defeat from Abeokuta. This was a Yoruba city/state which had been created by the Oyo Empire to protect refugees from Dahomey raids. Abeokuta was also responsible for assassinating Ghezo. The pressure from Britain, combined with the pressure from a strong neighbor, also weakened the failing Kingdom of Dahomey.

The war with France

Dahomey, already weakened by a failing slave trade and the threat of their Abeokuta neighbor, found itself in the eye of French colonial aspirations. France felt that it was losing out to Britain and Germany in the scramble for Africa, so it decided some Atlantic ports would be a good idea.

This led to some conflict encouraged by France, who wanted to provoke a struggle. The struggle culminated in the first and second Franco-Dahomean wars in which the last king of Dahomey, Béhanzin, was defeated and exiled.

Dahomey was annexed by French West Africa and became a colony of France. Dahomey gained its independence in 1958 as the Republic of Dahomey and became part of Benin in 1975. The Kingdom of Dahomey was officially over, but its traditions and culture are still an important tourist attraction in Benin.

The rise and fall of any kingdom always have a number of reasons. Dahomey's political and economic decline was a combination of changing global perspectives and needs and the pressures from stronger and more sophisticated countries like France. It was also part of a worldwide move towards the more ethical treatment of one's fellow man. Living in the darkest Africa and eating your enemies was no longer socially and morally acceptable. Neither, for that matter, was colonialism, but that only fell into disfavor a century later.

Chapter Eleven
Trivia from Popular perceptions of Dahomey

Movies and books have always loved the theme of the Amazon Dahomean warriors. Here are some of their favorite inclusions.

- The Dahomey kingdom was called "Black Sparta." The huge Amazon army consisted of nearly 6,000 all-female soldiers. The amazing exploits of these soldiers saw them being given that name which was quite a compliment because Spartans were very tough and fearless women warriors.

- Dahomey was a tiny insignificant kingdom situated in the northeastern part of what is now called Benin. The area used to be called "The Slave Coast." This is because so many enslaved Africans were taken captive and taken by slave ships to be sold to American cotton and other farmers.

- The Amazon soldiers carried deadly weapons called "the reapers." These sword-like weapons resembled three-foot-long razors. They were straight and deadly sharp, and the soldiers needed to use both hands to wield the blades.

- The Amazons women fought with their hands, knives, and clubs and wore no shoes. They were large, strong women and so fearsome that it was believed that they turned into men after killing their first victim.

- King Gezo, from 1818 to 1858, apparently complimented the gbeto hunters. One of them commented that she would have preferred a manhunt to a traditional hunt. The king decided to make the women hunters into a mighty army. He expanded their ranks to 6,000 soldiers.

- There has never been another all-woman army in full-time combat. The Dahomey Amazons were full-time soldiers.

- No one is quite sure where the Amazons came from. One "myth" is that they were all wives of a king from the 1500s. He weeded out the plain, ugly or barren ones and made them into an army to protect himself and his household.

- The Dahomey Amazons had huntress origins. One story from a French officer, which clearly has to be taken with a pinch of salt, is that 20 gbeto attacked a herd of 40 elephants, killed three, and took them back to feed the people.

- Dahomey soldiers were celibate. They married the king, but he never slept with them. This fuelled the rumor that they turned into men after their first kill. This story of the Dahomey Amazons has found a place in popular fiction as a role model for armies like The Unsullied in the Game of Thrones.

The Woman King

The movie The Woman King, released in September 2022, is a must-watch for those who love the fictional aspect of the Dahomey Amazons, which, although "based on fact," is just popular culture fact.

The movie has great reviews with a largely accurate historical plot, albeit with great artistic license. The geographical details and historical timeline are accurate, but the character specifics and the role of slavery are not. The characters are not historically accurate, especially the character of King Ghezo, who was not the benevolent and wise king the movie depicted him to be. He was defined as fiercely against the slave trade when in fact, quite the opposite was true.

Although excellently cast, Viola Davis, the lead actress, was not based on a historical figure.

So, while the movie was a great epic set in Africa, it certainly did not portray the Dahomeans as the bloodthirsty and ambitious slavers that history describes. Still, it's well worth watching, even if just for the magnificent scenery and scenes.

Chapter Twelve
Conclusion

The rise and fall of the Kingdom of Dahomey, besides being a riveting look into a fascinating period of history, gives us a deep look into one of the darkest and cruelest periods in human history and one which has had social and economic consequences to this day.

The Dahomeans were innovative and skillful people who could have been living a relatively peaceful pastoral life plowing their fields, harvesting their crops, and enjoying their lives as families and communities.

Instead, they found a market for one of the most despicable commodities ever, the trade in human flesh. Now, the Dahomeans were just one of many nations throughout history which has enslaved people, and there have been many traders of slaves at various times in history. Conquered people have traditionally been enslaved, but in this case, the sophisticated Western government-run infrastructure met the ambition and greed of the Dahomean royalty, and the consequences were dire for the population of Western Africa. At a time when an army of 6,000 was considered impressive, the mere fact that eight million people from Africa were taken from their homeland and enslaved in foreign lands, predominantly America, is startling and shocking.

The Dahomeans showed significant talents in art and culture and had an organized and efficient bureaucracy, but their progress was marred by their greed and ambition. They rose to power by conquest and war in their bid to increase their slave market, and they fell from power once their commodity was no longer required.

It's easy to look back from another time, however, and judge history from the perspective of the twenty-first century.

Although there are no physically enslaved people in the world anymore, there are still many exploited people and economic slaves, and the footprint of colonialism is still heavy in Africa, America, and many other countries.

We have the whole of history behind us, and we can gain perspective from it and learn the lessons that it can teach us. The world is still full of greedy and ambitious people who wish to exploit others, but we have the choice to decide how we want to live to protect our environment and respect the rights and safety of our fellow man. We can choose where to live and what path to follow. There's more freedom now than there ever has been, and it's up to us to use it wisely, learning from the past.

Chapter Thirteen
Discussion Question

A great number of ethical issues about slavery are raised. Who do you think should take the most blame? Those who provided the enslaved people or those who bought them? Justify your response.

Discussion Question

Vodou or Voodoo? This ancient religion has a very scary aspect to it. Is it justified or not?

Discussion Question

What do you think about the Amazon army of the Dahomeans?

Should women have been free to join the army? Was it discrimination or liberation?

Discussion Question

Colonialism brought about the final end to the Kingdom of Dahomey. What right did the colonial powers have to carve up Africa? Should they have left the Dahomeans alone to continue the traditional way of life?

Discussion Question

What's your take on cannibalism and human sacrifice? Is there a risk in imposing Western ideologies on other cultures? Yes or no?

Discussion Question

What aspects of Dahomean art did you find interesting? Was their art part of the fetish system? Justify your answer.

Discussion Question

What do you think about the amalgamation of Christianity and Vodou? Are they in any way compatible? Justify your answer.

Discussion Question

Do you think that modern filmmakers use too much artistic license when making films about controversial subjects? Do they impose Western ideology on their characters? Does this work for you? Explain your position.

ChapterFourteen
Quiz Question

1. **True/False:** The Dahomean Amazons were called the Mino. The name Amazon was given to them by Europeans. It came from Greek mythology.

2. **True/False:** King Ghezo was a kindly ruler who hated the slave trade. He tried to persuade his countrymen to abandon it. This was to no avail.

3. **True/False:** The French wanted to take land from Dahomey because they hated their cruel practices. The pope demanded that they do their Christian duty. It was their moral obligation.

4. **True/False:** The Dahomean warriors were not allowed to enjoy usual feminine activities. They could not have babies. Many of them were virgins.

5. **True/ False:** A modern fetishist is a type of witch doctor. They do not give medicine. They seek advice from the spirits.

6. **True/False:** The Dahomean Amazons were originally hunters. They impressed the King so much that he made them warriors. He also expanded their numbers.

7. **True/False:** The Vodou Religion started in Haiti. It spread to Africa. No one is sure how it arrived on African shores.

8. **True/ False:** The Dahomean Amazons were fearless fighters. They used weapons or hand-to-hand combat. They even used their teeth if nothing else was available.

Quiz Answer

1. True

2. False: King Ghezo was a cruel king. He refused to abandon the slave trade. The British and his neighbors tried to persuade him to do so.

3. False: The French felt left out of the scramble for Africa. They wanted to compete with England and Germany. There were no ethics involved.

4. True

5. True

6. True

7. False: The Vodou Religion came from Africa. It was spread to Haiti by slaves. It's very popular in both countries.

8. True

Bibliography

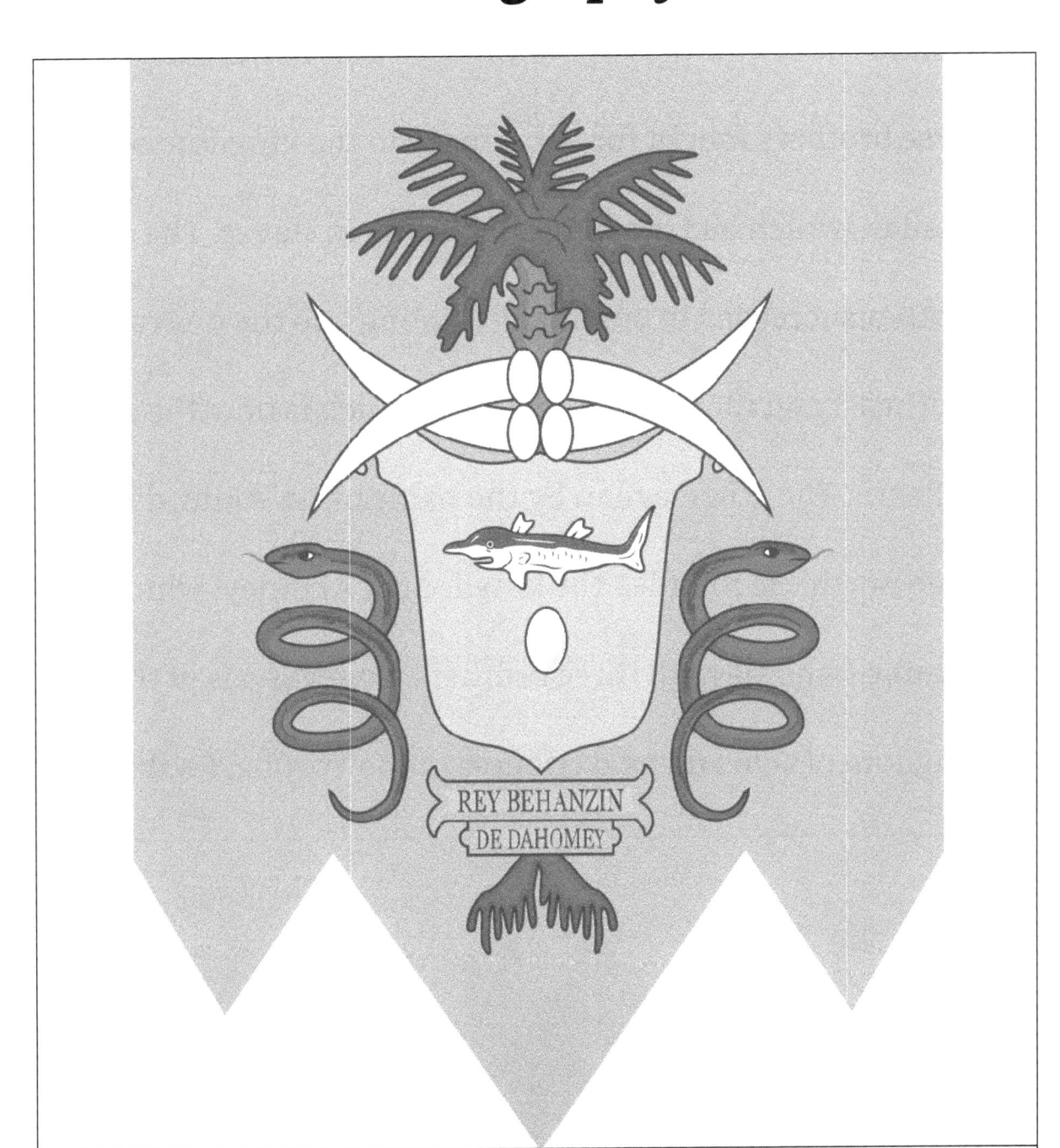

The Royal Banner (1889-1892)

Dahomey was a historical kingdom situated in West Africa. It was highly successful during the 1700s and 1800s. It's now part of the southern Benin region. The traditional story around the beginnings of Dahomey is that in the early 1600s, three brothers fought for supremacy in the kingdom of Alladah, which had grown rich, trading in slaves. The one brother succeeded in ousting his siblings, so the one traveled southeast and founded Porto-Novo, which is now the capital of Benin. The other, a man by the name of Do-Aklin, decided to go north. He founded the kingdom of Abomey, which later became Dahomey. All three brothers were vassals of the kingdom of Oyo and paid tributes to the Yoruba. **(Wikipedia)**

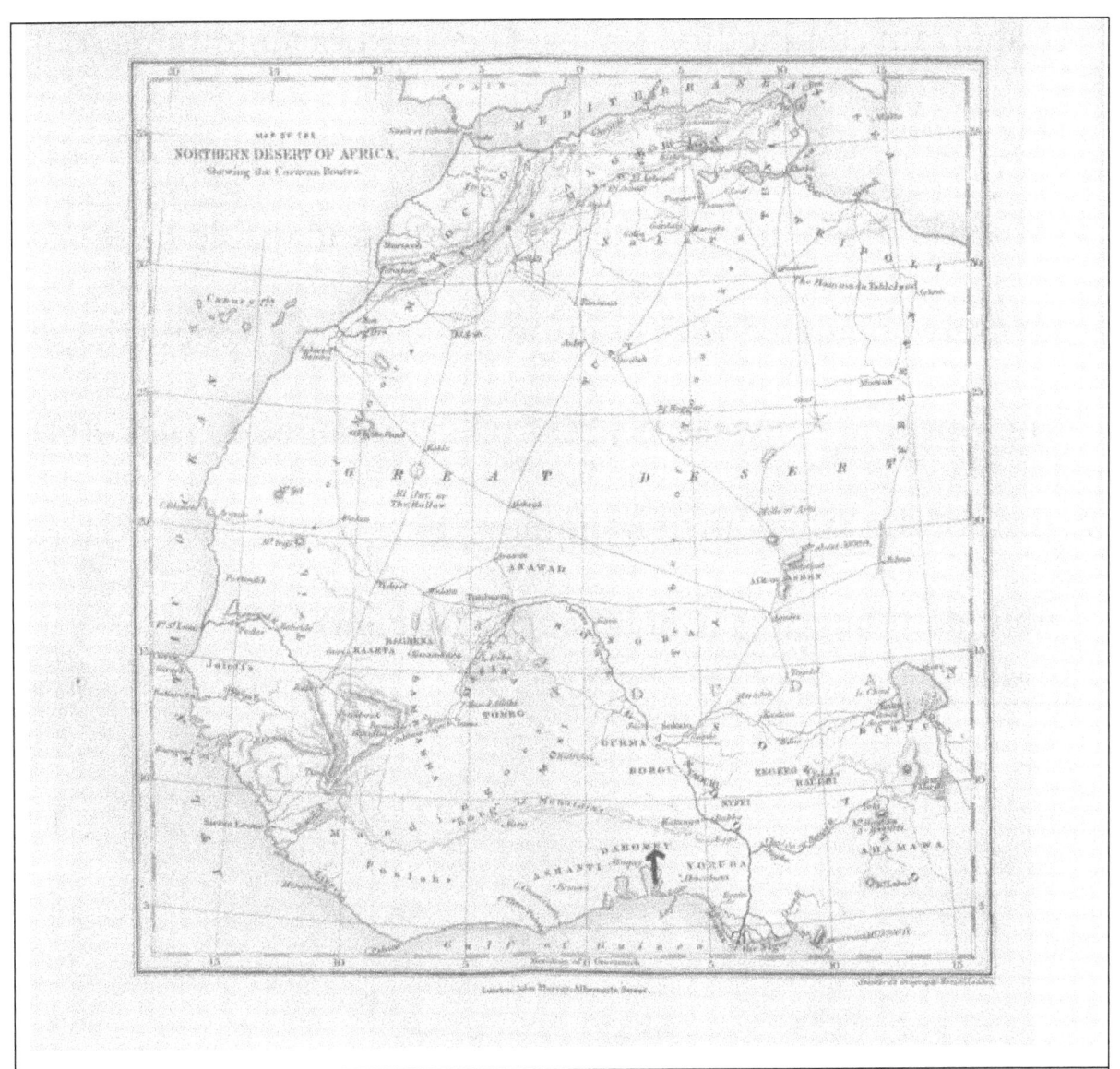

Geography

Dahomey was founded on the Abomey Plateau by one of the chiefs of the Fon people in the early 1600s. By the 1700s, it had become a significant regional power. It expanded to the South and conquered important cities like Whydah on the Atlantic Coast. This guaranteed unhindered trade for its most important commodity, slaves. The Atakora Mountains run through part of Dahomey, and it stretches down to the Atlantic Ocean. It's very hot and humid and would have been densely populated with wildlife, which as in all countries of the world, are now largely restricted to Game reserves. At the time of the Kingdom of Dahomey, there would have been abundant hunting. **(Guidebooktolife.com)**

The Amazons of Dahomey

The Mino were named Amazons by visiting Europeans. These were a group of women warriors from Greek mythology. They were portrayed in many ancient legends and celebrated in epic poems. They were a group of female warriors and hunters, superior in fitness and skill to men and able to beat them in areas of combat, horse riding, strength, and agility. Their society was not open to any males, and they killed any sons born to them or, if they were fortunate, returned them to their fathers. They raised their daughters to be warriors.

They only had brief sexual interludes with men for the purpose of procreation. (**Guidebooktolife.com**)

1528. - Afrique Occidentale Dahomey - Jeunes féticheuses

A Vodou Ritual

The main aim of Vodou is to serve the spirits and perform various devotions to appease or please the spirits and get particular favors like wealth, health, and protection. During the possession rituals, trances are also common, and the devotee may drink or eat some ritual foods. Cannibalism is not unknown in some cases, but cannibalistic rituals are more often performed as a show of power. The devotees perform specific dances and might perform athletic or sexual feats and medical cures. The ritual dances, trances, and other aspects of the possession ceremony are meant to restore and refine the balance between spirits and people. **(Wikipedia)**

Slavery in Dahomey

We can't write about the Kingdom of Dahomey without looking at the broader picture of the terrible scourge of slavery. A large reason for the collapse of the Kingdom of Dahomey was the end of international slavery in the mid-

1800s. Slavery had been far more lucrative for the militant kingdom than the palm oil trade, which replaced it. Slavery, however, was an immoral, cruel and inhumane way to make a living, and the Dahomeans deserved to lose that terrible livelihood. It is impossible to feel saddened in any way by the demise of the Kingdom of Dahomey. (**slaveryimages.org**)

The Colonizers

Dahomey huddled along Africa's Atlantic coast, had been a sporadic source of attention from European colonialists since Portuguese and Dutch explorers noted the Gold Coast in the 1500s and 1600s. Dahomey operated a successful slave trade of major interest to the colonists. By 1887, the Dutch had moved on, but the Portuguese still maintained loose control over the exporting of Dahomey palm oil.

(https://www.smithsonianmag.com/)

The Woman King

The movie The Woman King, released in September 2022, is a must-watch for those who love the fictional aspect of the Dahomey Amazons, which, although "based on fact," is just popular culture fact. The movie has great reviews with a largely accurate historical plot, albeit with great artistic license. The geographical details and historical timeline are accurate, but the character specifics and the role of slavery are not. The characters are not historically accurate, especially the character of King Ghezo, who was not the benevolent and wise king the movie depicted him as being. He was defined as fiercely against the slave trade when in fact, quite the opposite was true.

Although excellently cast, Viola Davis, the lead actress, was not based on a historical figure. (slate.com)

Bonus Downloads

*Get Free Books with **Any Purchase**History Hub*

Every purchase comes with a FREE download!

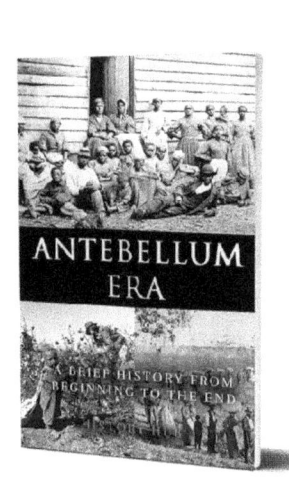

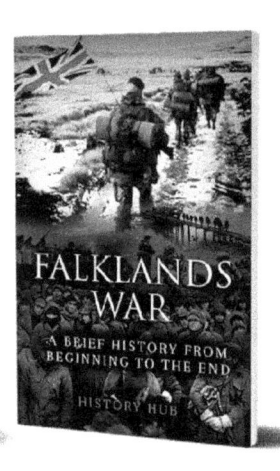

Thank You For Reading

As an independent publisher

with a tiny marketing budget

we rely on readers, like you.

If you're receiving help from this book,

would you please take a moment to write a brief review?

We really appreciate it.

Milton Keynes UK
Ingram Content Group UK Ltd.
UKHW012307141124
451150UK00012B/222